Christmas Contrasts

Christmas Contrasts

Poems That Explore Different Ways to Understand Christmas

S T Kimbrough, Jr.

FOREWORD BY
C. Michael Hawn

RESOURCE *Publications* · Eugene, Oregon

CHRISTMAS CONTRASTS
Poems That Explore Different Ways to Understand Christmas

Resource Publications
An Imprint of Wipf and Stock Publishers
199 W. 8th Ave., Suite 3
Eugene, OR 97401

www.wipfandstock.com

PAPERBACK ISBN: 979-8-3852-0467-0
HARDCOVER ISBN: 979-8-3852-0468-7
EBOOK ISBN: 979-8-3852-0469-4

VERSION NUMBER 10/30/23

Translated text from front cover image: "Please offer shelter, a room, or a restaurant ticket, thank you."

Contents

Foreword

Christianity is a paradoxical faith perspective. Convergent ideas that seem untrue or impossible when placed in juxtaposition become imbued with a richness of meaning that surpasses any single assertion. Though the paradoxes of faith are evident during any season of the Christian year, it is perhaps in our preparations for and celebration of Christmas that these are most apparent. Contrasts of abundance and scarcity, togetherness and isolation, and contentment and misery coexist. *Christmas Contrasts* explores these paradoxes in a way that enhances our understanding of the Incarnation—the one who saves us (Jesus) and abides with us (Emmanuel).

S T Kimbrough draws upon a wealth of theological training, cross-cultural encounters, and familial experiences to weave together threads of meaning that comfort, challenge, and concern. "17. Christmas Candles" brings an autobiographical warmth of past memories. "19. An Unjust Palestine" challenges us to recall that the oppressed during the time of Christ's birth have become the oppressors in modern Palestine. "24. Alone at Christmas" forefronts our concern for those around us who live in isolation during a season of communal festivity.

Rather than treating the theme polemically, the author chooses the lyrical art form of the poem. Kimbrough's purpose is not to persuade or convince us but to invite us to remember, reconsider, and recognize the deeper realities of the coming of the One who offers consolation to those who suffer and struggle and gives meaning to our existence. The purpose of these poems is not to feel good but to feel again and live into the contrasting

paradoxes of our faith. Savor these poems throughout the season
and allow them to guide you into the richness of living into the
paradoxes of the Incarnation.

C. Michael Hawn

University Distinguished Professor *Emeritus* of Church Music
Southern Methodist University, Dallas, Texas

Introduction

1. Contrasts

How interesting are most contrasts,
    they're often opposites, you see.
One may be constant, lasts and lasts,
    one may last temporarily.

The mountains, valleys aren't the same,
    they're contrasts to one another.
Though sheep and goats may be quite tame,
    they're hardly sister and brother.

There's high and low, there's up and down;
    There's fertile soil and arid land
and curved and straight streets in a town.
    Sometimes we sit, sometimes we stand.

There's left and right, forward and back;
    there's round about and straight ahead.
There's morning's blue sky, night time's black;
    there's what's alive and what is dead.

Contrasts we cannot live without;
    they color language, stories, art.
They're here to stay without a doubt.
    Enjoy them, take each one to heart.

I am struck by the contrasts of Christmas some of which are troubling, while others are comforting. The poem with which I begin this book of poems juxtaposes some of these. Some are contrasts of the past and present and others are contrasts within past and present time frames. They evoke vivid images, many of which we know well. Some are pleasant and others are disturbing. How do we deal with the reality of many of these contrasts that emphasize our failure to grasp the meaning of Christmas in such a way that we live the message of peace and goodwill? Each Advent and Christmas season is a season of hope and failure. The hope of peace and goodwill inaugurated in the birth of the Christ Child is contrasted with the failure of his followers to bring to realization the peace and goodwill of which the angels sing. Is it possible that a careful look at the often extreme contrasts of Christmas can help us better understand its meaning and how its meaning can be fulfilled in humankind today? This is what I will explore in this book of poems.

2. Christmas Contrasts

Brightly decorated homes,
hovel dwellings of the poor.

Well-dressed, holiday shoppers,
street children dressed in rags.

Bright tree lights and baubles,
Ukrainian homes without power.

Joyful, well-fed carolers,
hungry, crying children.

Christ Child born in a stall,
poinsettia-graced churches.

Shepherds from the fields,
wise men from the East.

Wealth of Christmas industry,
poverty of the Christ-Child.

Gift-laden Christmas trees,
homeless children with nothing.

Purchase of Christmas gifts,
God's gift of the Christ-Child.

Economic success of Christmas sales,
God's concern for the well-being of all.

Perhaps one of the most puzzling contrasts from the past is how a segment of the powerful Roman empire became threatened by a non-military power that would rule in the heart (see "5. From 63 B.C."). Rome's rulers and administrative leaders are not interested in hearing of a "Prince of Peace" who will release people from bondage, hatred, prejudice, and greed.[1] It is radically offensive to Roman leadership that Rome's subjects—

. . . come from the fields, from the East,
the humble, the wisest of wise,
to worship a child of the least
from whom love for all will arise.[2]

It is simply unimaginable to Rome that "A Palestinian Jewish Boy" could become such a threat to the empire. Rome's goal was survival at any cost, especially the exploitation of its subjects. Yet there emerges a message through this Palestinian Jewish boy that will take the Middle East at a breath-taking pace. He "showed how in loving sacrifice / goodwill can be a worthwhile price."

1. "3. A Newborn Child."
2. "7. Of Abraham's Lineage."

Rome desired no message of the salvation of a people. It *was* the people's salvation. But "New hope is born on Christmas night / when Rome had kept it out of sight."[3] "Still many placed their hope in Rome / while others hoped in One to come." Here the contrast between the status quo and the future is vividly apparent.

An amazing contrast in the Bethlehem story is the notoriety the mother of the awaited Child will enjoy in the future. A teenage Palestinian girl named Mary will be known by a different name in the future. She is not just Mary the mother of Jesus, rather

> *Theotokos,* Mary is called,
> holy "Mother of God,"
> a name now spread abroad:
> for ages has the church enthralled.[4]

What a contrast: this unknown, Palestinian girl of humble origin enjoys a place of highest esteem in the history of the Christian Church.

While there are in the New Testament account of the Bethlehem Child elements of strong contrast, such as the visitors to the Holy Family, shepherds and wise men from the East, there is another interesting one in the shepherds' visit itself. They come to visit a newborn Child who will one day be called the Shepherd of the sheep: "A Shepherd is born who will care for the sheep." The "cared for sheep" come to visit the "caretaker of the sheep."

An interesting contrast are the journeys of the wise men, namely, their journey to Bethlehem and their return to the East from whence they came. Their first journey guided by a star leads them to the place where the Child is born. Their return, however, follows a different route, emphasizing that those who follow the newborn Child must often go different paths to avoid the evils of the world.

There are not only Christmas contrasts in the biblical story but in the present celebration of Christmas:

3. "9. Messiah Love."
4. "11. Mother of God."

> Though Christmas comes but once a year,
>   it never is the same.
> Its message we each year may hear
>   and know the Christ-Child's name.
> If no one demonstrates goodwill,
>   and no one acts for peace,
> How will we know it's Christmas still
>   and love for all increase?[5]

The title of the poem from which this stanza comes is "Never the Same and Yet the Same," the ultimate contrast. The message of peace and goodwill is constantly the same, but the contrasting question remains—When will peace and goodwill be realized? Even as modern followers of the Christ Child follow the star to Bethlehem year after year, they learn

> It leads to peace and goodwill,
> even when the path thwarts our will,
> even when it leads to the least,
> where God's own love is released.
> In a baby of the poor
> [we find] love that will endure.[6]

What of the contrast between the birth of the Christ Child and the birth of every other human being. Of course, there is the contrast of human and divine, but

> Every time we hear the welcome news:
>   "Your child's been born and all is well,"
> remember God a birth did choose
>   salvation's story of love to tell.[7]

What a contrast in the way we sing of Christmas and present reality.

> Why is it we sing "Silent Night"
>   the night the angels sing?
> We long for quiet, inner sight
>   that silence still can bring.[8]

5. "6. Never the Same and Yet the Same."
6. "13. Following a Star."
7. "15. Tidings of Great Joy."
8. "16. Silents Nights."

There was probably little silence in an animal stall the night of the Christ Child's birth. Yet, we imagine it as silent and holy. We still sing "Silent Night, holy night" in contrast to the blazing force of guns, bombs, and drones in many parts of the world. Yet—

> We ponder words of peace, goodwill,
>   in awe think of a birth
> that might in humankind instill
>   a love throughout the earth.

There is a hidden contrast in the Christmas carols we sing. We may know the words and the music, and yet there are times when one may seem less important than the other, though we may be completely unaware of it. Words and music are both a complement and a contrast.

> A melody can soothe the soul
> around the world from pole to pole.
> . . .
> Without the words the tune can lift
> our spirits; this is music's gift.[9]

As Christmas comes again and again, year after year, perhaps the contrasts will endure because of human imperfection. Perhaps this is why we keep burning candles, hoping that somehow light will illumine the darkness of the world in which we live.

> When Christmas candles burn once more,
> oh may their light in us restore
> the angel's message of goodwill
> and peace for which we're praying still.[10]

One of the greatest contrasts of all having to do with the Christmas story is the contrast between the Bethlehem of biblical times and the Bethlehem of the twenty-first century. Today it is a walled-in city cutting off Christian and Muslim communities from Israel's population. The wall is to protect the Israeli's from

9. "17. Christmas Carols."
10. "18. Christmas Candles."

Christians, Muslims, their so-called acts of violence, and misdirected beliefs about human and land rights.

> "O little town of Bethlehem,"
> how walled-in now you lie!
> We faintly hear the angels' hymn,
> though Christian voices try.
> The Christians left in Palestine
> are now so very few.
> Their population's in decline:
> rights gone that once they knew.[11]

So let us sing a new carol of the contrasts of Christmas.

> Let silence reign throughout the earth,
> let Christmas morning break.
> Let there be peace at this new birth;
> let countries war forsake.
>
> Let silence on a Christmas morn
> fill souls with quiet peace,
> for love upon this morn was born,
> divine the masterpiece.
>
> This child's born of inclusive love
> to spread to humankind;
> it's spirit's gentle as a dove
> to rest on every mind.
>
> As this Child to the earth once came,
> "Come now, inclusive love."
> This prayer we pray always the same:
> "Descend, oh peaceful dove."[12]

The poems of the last section in the book address family life at Christmas, which has interesting contrasts too. First of all, there

---

11. "21. A Christmas Song, Old and New"
12. "19. A Silent Christmas Morn."

is the obvious contrast between those who have family and those
who do not at Christmas or any other time. They

> have lost a spouse or dearest friend,
> [and] never thought things would so end.
>
> . . .
>
> How comforting Emmanuel,
> "God with us"—yes, these words do well
> Reminding us we're not alone.
> Still if someone would telephone,
> at Christmas I'd not be alone.[13]

Family members tend to think of one another at Christmas
time. Some families have special ways of gift giving. Some draw
names so that each person receives at least one gift. Others ex-
change funny gifts by a variety of methods. But what a contrast it
is indeed for the person whose last thought is giving or receiving
a gift at Christmas.

> I'd like to be in a clean place
> where I would see a friendly face.
>
> On Christmas morning that would be
> the gift that I'd most want for me.[14]

What a contrast to the family gathered around its lavishly deco-
rated tree surrounded by a mountain of presents on Christmas
morning.

What people anticipate or do not expect at the Christmas
season is as diverse as the circumstances in which they find
themselves.

> Who wants, needs, waits this year,
> this year at Christmas time?
> Rich with or without cheer,
> and those without a dime.[15]

---

13. "25. Alone at Christmas."
14. "26. The Gift That I Want Most."
15. "27. To Want, Need, Wait."

Let there be no illusions, however, contrasts occur as well within families with enduring Christmas traditions. A family grows and expands. Children become parents and grandparents, and the traditions often change from generation to generation. "Our family's changed across the years, / but each tradition always cheers."[16] We sometimes wonder how we can hold on to traditions passed down from previous generations.

Christmas memories can also create contrasts that may make us very happy or sad. As the song "Toyland" says of the wondrous days of childhood they "can ne'er return again." The contrast with the present in which we find ourselves can be overwhelmingly sad, especially if we have romanticized a childhood Christmas as so extraordinary that all others will be a grave letdown.

The reality is that some contrasts of Christmas, especially within families, are as different as the people who celebrate the birth of the Bethlehem Child. "Some dance and sing in bright array, / while others simply sing and pray."[17] The contrasts of Christmas can be a source of tremendous joy but also of sadness. However, learning from these contrasts can strengthen the wonder of the celebration of Christmas. We celebrate a Child whose birth and life fill the gap between the contrasts we often create or those that may occur quite naturally in the course of life. He brings together the contrasts of joy and sadness by exemplifying the love and care of every person through inclusive love! With this kind of love we learn to turn the contrasts of Christmas into wondrous jubilation!

16. "29. Tradition(s)."
17. "37. Overwhelming Joy."

Contrasts of Christ's Birth

3. A Newborn Child

Mary, Joseph appear,
for Mary's time is near.
Yet no one takes them in,
not even at an inn.
Resigned they find a stall
with animals, that's all.
And there she birthed her boy,
whose destiny is joy:
"To all—joy, peace, goodwill!"
hear shepherds on a hill,
sung by an angel choir.
God's hope and God's desire,
found in a newborn son,
in this small child are won.
The shepherds rush to him
in nearby Bethlehem.
And Wise Men from afar
soon follow a bright star
that rests above the place
of God's lasting embrace
of all throughout the world
with love to all unfurled.
This child will become known
for love that will be shown
as love for every soul,
love that alone makes whole.

What name will this child bear,
to be known everywhere?
Jesus, the Prince of Peace,
whose love gives all release,
release from slavery
and inhumanity,
from hatred, prejudice,
from greed and avarice.
But who will follow him,
this child of Bethlehem?

Contrasts of Names

Jesus (Active Presence) and
Emmanuel (Eternal Presence)

4. Names of the Holy Child

The child named Jesus at his birth,
    was also called Emmanuel.
Those names resound around the earth,
    as prophets, gospel writers tell.

What are the meanings of these names?—
    The one who heals and one who saves
is Jesus, who peace, goodwill frames,
    who brings release and frees the slaves.

"God with us" is Emmanuel,
    forever here, always the same.
The One who comes with us to dwell,
    and saves the sinner through his name.

Then speak these names with reverence,
    each name regard with holiness.
Each name reveals the evidence
    of God's intent: all souls to bless.

This holy Child will save and heal
    the sick, the blind, all who are lost.
This Child brings love all souls can feel,
    a love that gives at any cost.

Contrasts of Roman Rule

5. From 63 B.C.E.

Roman rule of Palestine
o'ershadowed all the land
that has been known as "holy."

But nothing Roman rulers did
could be averred as holy
with iron, merciless ruling hands.

We know the name Vespasian,
last ruler of the Flavian dynasty
and of King Herod, Pontius Pilate.

This little land, strategic between
three continents, became known
for things other than Roman rule.

It became known for a different
kind of non-military power
that would rule in the heart.

Within the Palestinian realm
Rome became threatened
by the power of the human heart.

A Child born in Bethlehem
was such a threat that Herod
desperately wanted him dead.

The escape of the Child
made possible an invasion,
an invasion of love in hearts.

This invasion continues still,
no force has yet quelled it.
And the Christmas Child's reborn,

reborn with each year's memory
of his birth, childhood, wisdom,
outreach, love, and sacrifice for all.

Contrasts of the Meaning of Christmas

6. Never the Same and Yet the Same

Though Christmas comes but once a year,
    it never is the same.
Its message we each year may hear
    and know the Christ-Child's name.
If no one demonstrates goodwill,
    and no one acts for peace,
How will we know it's Christmas still
    and love for all increase?

This year will we hear songs of joy,
    will we yet carols sing?
Will we still think that Mary's boy
    is why the church bells ring?
Yes, Christmas each year bears Christ's name
    and peace, goodwill proclaims.
This lasting message is the same
    in all of earth's domains.

So Christmas comes and Christmas goes;
    it may be just routine.
Should we then ask at each year's close:
    What does this Christmas mean?
We sing of peace and mercy mild,
    and love for all on earth.
All three are found in Christ the Child,
    all three give life its worth.

Contrasts of Christ's Lineage

7. Of Abraham's Lineage

Of Abraham's lineage he was,
    Child Jesus born in Bethlehem,
who cent'ries long gives humans pause
    to ponder and reflect on him.

Foreshadowing his purpose, cause,
    come humble shepherds from the field,
who from their labors quickly pause
    to learn what's by this birth revealed.

Foreshadowing his cause as well
    come men of wisdom from the East,
who follow star-beams whose light fell
    upon a child born of the least.

They come from the fields, from the East,
    the humble, the wisest of wise,
to worship a child of the least
    from whom love for all will arise.

Contrasts of Christ's Palestinian-Jewish Heritage

8. A Palestinian Jewish Boy

In Palestine a Jewish boy
was born with songs of angel joy.
Some local shepherds heard the hymn
the angels sang near Bethlehem.
Help us to live in harmony,
God's purpose for humanity.

They sang of peace and of goodwill
with which this child all hearts could fill,
not as a governor or king,
but one who love to hearts would bring.
Help us to live in harmony,
God's purpose for humanity.

Imagine that in Palestine
in this child peace, goodwill combine
with love for all of humankind—
all this in Palestine to find!
Help us to live in harmony,
God's purpose for humanity.

This Jewish boy became a man
and in his wonderful life-span
showed how in loving sacrifice
goodwill can be a worthwhile price.
Help us to live in harmony,
God's purpose for humanity.

Contrasts of Hope and Hopelessness

9. Messiah Love

New hope is born on Christmas night
though Rome had kept it out of sight.
With taxes, homage paid to Rome,
one could be robbed of shelter, home.
It's no surprise that people pray,
O come, Messiah, come this day.

Still many placed their hope in Rome,
while others hoped in One to come:
Messiah, Counselor of Peace,
through love would powers of Rome decrease.
Messiah's hope is peace, goodwill,
a hope that teaches all love's skill.

A child was born in Bethlehem,
a birth hailed by an angels' hymn.
Mysterious is the wonder still
that in a child of holy will
the world through love can now be changed,
though hosts remain from love estranged.

Messiah-Child salvation brings,
but not through mighty power of kings.
Salvation brings us changing hearts
and love to all in all earth's parts.
The angels' song is our reply:
"Glory to God, to God on high."

Contrasts of Jesus' Relatives

10. Remembering *Ein Keram*[18]

Ein Keram is a lovely place
    where blessed Mary's cousin dwelled.
Elizabeth her name, by grace
    two women miracles beheld.

These cousins blessed with love divine
    bore children who would change the world:
sons John and Jesus, men divine
    through whom love's banner was unfurled.

This love prepares in every place
    to give of self and know no loss;
turns hate to love in every race,
    though love led Jesus to a cross.

18. *Ein Keram* is a historic mountain village southwest of Jerusalem that is thought to be the birthplace of John the Baptist, son of Elizabeth, a relative of Mary, the mother of Jesus.

Contrasts of Young Mary and *Theotokos*[19]

11. Mother of God

When Mary looked into the face
   of her newly born child,
    was there a chance he smiled
as she held him in warm embrace?
Did Mary feel what mothers feel
    when they first glimpse their own:
    he's of my flesh, my bone,
and of my breast takes his first meal?

She'd heard the annunciation
    from an angelic voice.
    Was this birth of her choice?
How would others see her station?
Theotokos, Mary is called,
    holy "Mother of God,"
    a name now spread abroad
for ages has the church enthralled.

Jesus, name of the child she bore,
    means one who comes to save,
    for which his life he gave,
that love into all hearts would pour.
Self-giving love he lived and taught
    and died to show us how
    for all love to avow,
and thus to live the way we ought.

19. This is the Greek word translated "Mother of God," a title for Mary, the mother of Jesus, in Eastern Christianity.

Contrasts of the Shepherds
and *The* Shepherd

Luke 2:15–16, "When the angels had left them and gone into heaven, the shepherds said to one another, 'Let us go now to Bethlehem and see this thing that has taken place, which the Lord has made known to us.' So they went with haste and found Mary and Joseph, and the child lying in a manger."

12. The Birth of a Shepherd

How strange, shepherds leave their flocks,
quite irresponsible some would say,
for sheep will stray when left alone.
Their guardians, protectors from harm,
hear an angel message, and depart.

At lambing time they're always at hand
to tend to the birthing of new lambs.
At other times they rarely leave their flocks;
the dangers are too great, but now they leave
their sheep in the fields without care.

It is another birthing they leave to attend,
the one of which the angels sang,
a Shepherd is born who will care for all sheep,
those that stray and those that do not.
They wonder what the future will hold.

Contrasts of Purpose and Fulfillment

13. Following a Star

Are there yet stars to follow
a Sun-god or Apollo?
Are there yet eastern Wise Men
that guide us to an amen
of life's purpose and meaning,
each day we should be gleaning?

A star we need as a guide,
a star to help us decide
the best path that we should take
each morning when we awake.
From eastern Wise Men we learn
a guiding star not to spurn.

It leads to peace and goodwill,
ev'n when the path thwarts our will,
ev'n when it leads to the least,
where God's own love is released.
A Child who's born of the poor
shares love, that will last, endure.

Like Wise Men we should be wise
to follow this star, the prize:
it leads to goodwill, love, peace,
which Christ, this Child, will increase.
So, follow Bethlehem's star:
make peace, goodwill where you are.

Contrasts of Promised Wisdom and Fulfilled Wisdom

14. Wisdom from the East

Ancient Wise Men of the East
spoke of the coming of wisdom
in a forthcoming child's birth.
Years later other Wise Men
from the East went in quest
of the child who'd been foretold.

Guided by a heavenly star,
they seek the newborn Child,
whose wisdom makes wise.
With their eyes upon the star,
they follow miles upon miles
until they find the Child.

Known as Emmanuel, God with us,
and also Wonderful Counselor,
and above all, the Prince of Peace,
these eastern sages were wise
to seek such a Child long ago.
Each Christmas reveals their wisdom.

Contrasts of Christ's Birth and Every Child's Birth

15. Tidings of Great Joy

To shepherds an angel once said,
    "I bring you good news of great joy."
These words around the world have spread
    the news of Mary's newborn boy.

All parents gladly hear this said
    when children of their own are born.
A father stands by mother's bed,
    through a long night until the morn.

Birth is the wondrous way all come
    into the world to live on earth.
For humankind this is the sum
    of what imparts their human worth.

Perhaps here's why God chooses birth
    to enter life like everyone.
Like every other child on earth
    the God-Child's birth is also done.

Each time we hear the welcome news:
    "Your child's been born and all is well,"
remember God a birth did choose
    salvation's love story to tell.

God's story of love in Mary's son
    begins anew when he is born,
for "Jesus" means salvation's won,
    and evil of its power is shorn.

Contrasts of Silence and the Angels' Song

16. Silent Nights

Why is it we sing "Silent Night"
　　the night the angels sing?
We long for quiet, inner sight
　　that silence still can bring.

We ponder words of peace, goodwill,
　　in awe think of a birth
that might in humankind instill
　　a love throughout the earth.

In Bethlehem love born that night
　　can capture minds and hearts,
and help us wonder if we might
　　spread love to all earth's parts.

This Child is born love's greatest source
　　for all of humankind.
This Child's love is the greatest force:
　　in one all hearts to bind.

Contrasts of Words and Music

17. Christmas Carols

We hear a certain tune we know
and sense its old familiar flow,
for it belongs to Christmas time;
we may ev'n know the words and rhyme.
Sometimes nostalgic we may be
about a carol's memory:
a fav'rite one our mothers sang,
or one played when the church bells rang.

A carol's tune can make us feel
that Christmas spirit's very real.
A melody can soothe the soul,
around the world, from pole to pole.
No matter, music's language, style,
it makes the life we live worthwhile.
It isn't just the words alone,
the tune has magic all its own.

Without the words the tune can lift
our spirits; this is music's gift.
The words may tell us Christ is born
and humankind is not forlorn,
if all by mutual love will live
and selflessly this love will give.
For thus the Christ Child lived and gave
his life of love the world to save.

Contrasts of Light and Darkness

18. Christmas Candles

Our Christmas candles burn once more,
the joys of Christmas to restore.
The largest one we light each year,
I'm told my grandma brought it here.
Her father molded it from wax,
so long ago it has some cracks.
And yet its flames still glow and shine;
Mom says one day it will be mine.
The red and green ones are my choice;
their dancing flames seem to rejoice.
The small white ones go on our tree;
their holders came from Germany.
An Advent wreath adorns a stand,
that came from Germany's Rhineland.
Four candles in the wreath recall,
as each one flickers on the wall,
that week by week the Advent light
leads us to Bethl'hem's starry night,
on which a Child of light was born,
the reason why there's Christmas morn.
Some shepherds were led by the light
to Bethlehem on Christmas night.
They also heard an angels' hymn
that beckoned them to Bethlehem:
Glory to God, to God on high,
Glory to God, for God is nigh.

Light led Wise Men to Bethlehem
to meet the Child praised in the hymn,
who brings peace and goodwill to earth,
God's gift to all in this child's birth.
When Christmas candles burn once more,
O may their light in us restore
the angel's message of goodwill
and peace for which we're praying still.

Contrasts of God's Silence and World Unrest

19. A Silent Christmas Morn

Let silence reign throughout the earth,
    let Christmas morning break.
Let there be peace at this new birth;
    let countries war forsake.

Let silence on a Christmas morn
    fill souls with quiet peace,
for love upon this morn was born,
    divine the masterpiece.

This child's born of inclusive love
    to spread to humankind;
its spirit's gentle as a dove
    to rest on every mind.

As this Child to the earth once came,
    "Come now, inclusive love."
This prayer we pray always the same:
    "Descend, O peaceful dove."

Contrasts of Jew and Non-Jew

20. An Unjust Palestine

To Palestinians in Israel now,
    in Israel's twisted view,
all equal rights will disallow
    but not of every Jew.
The Palestinians have a fate,
    a fate that could be changed,
if Israel's apartheid state
    for justice were exchanged.

The Christians left in Palestine
    are now so very few.
Their population's in decline:
    rights gone that they once knew.
The Palestinian people there,
    Christian, Muslim they be,
lead daily lives grossly unfair
    denied true liberty.

Contrasts of Past and Present 1

21. A Christmas Song, Old and New

"O little town of Bethlehem,"[20]
    how walled-in now you lie!
We faintly hear the angels' hymn,
    though Christian voices try.
The Christians left in Palestine
    are now so very few.
Their population's in decline,
    rights gone that they once knew.

"O little town of Bethlehem,"
    with settlers all around,
two bypass roads were made for them
    so they can miss the town.
Of Jesus' birth we still can hear,
    though walls, check-points prevail.
One message still is very clear:
    God's love will never fail.

---

20. This is the first line of a familiar Christmas carol by Phillips Brooks (1835–1893).

Contrasts of Past and Present 2

22. What Shall We Sing in Bethlehem?

What shall we sing in Bethlehem,
    the place where Christ was born?
Can we not find a Christmas hymn
    that overcomes the scorn
of those who built a giant wall
    around the entire town?
Yes, we can join in one and all,
    for love's the Christmas crown.

Love is the crown the Christ Child wears;
    the crown within the heart.
Love is the crown of all his heirs,
    in his love all take part.
No walls encircle Christmas love
    except walls of our hearts.
No force, no power is above
    the love this child imparts.

We sing God's love is not confined
    by walls or cowardice.
We sing this love's not cheap nor blind,
    nor harmed by prejudice.
In Bethlehem God's love is crowned,
    crowned for all time and space.
God's love for all earth's souls is found
    in every land and race.

Contrasts of the Christmas Song

23. "All Glory Be to God on High"

"All glory be to God on high,"
    we sing with angels, shepherds, kings,
who've come to worship God who's nigh,
    and learn of love the Christ Child brings.
The song continues ages long
    and shares with us the message still:
that God is love, the angels' song,
    that love is God's eternal will.

Did mother Mary sing that night
    as she held Jesus to her breast?
Did she the angels' song recite
    that hope for peace, goodwill expressed?
Perhaps she hummed a melody
    and gently nursed her newborn son.
But surely she could not foresee
    salvation for the world begun.

What joy we have at Christmas time
    when news of God's love fills the air,
and carols sung in joyous rhyme
    give us a sense that we are there.
We're present at the Savior's birth
    surrounded by the angel throng,
whose praise resounds around the earth
    and has become our Christmas song.

Contrasts of the Powerful
and the Powerless

24. Powerless Rome

The power of Rome, though broad in scope
had left its subjects without hope.
It ruled them with an iron fist
and would not anyone assist
with health or food or infant care;
its gross taxation was unfair.

To hear of one born of goodwill,
ideas of peace in all instill,
aroused within King Herod ire
along with a perverse desire
to find the Child and have him killed,
at least he thought Rome was so skilled.

This newborn Child of Peace he thought
could soon be found, a lesson taught:
Rome is in power, no Prince of Peace
could reign and his own power increase.
But this new reign was in the heart
and there it would have its fresh start.

So Bethlehem's young-infant born
meant Rome would be of power shorn,
not governmental power as such,
but power authorities can't touch.
Through this Child's love, peace, and goodwill,
the world is benefiting still.

Contrasts of Aloneness at Christmas

25. Alone at Christmas

Who is alone at Christmas time?—
the millions who in every clime,
have lost a spouse or dearest friend,
who never thought things would so end.
They will not decorate a tree;
they'll think, "Oh no, not just for me."
They'll hear some Christmas carols sung
and hear the church bells when they're rung.

They know the Christmas story's truth;
they've heard it each year since their youth.
How comforting Emmanuel,
"God with us"—yes, these words do well,
do well to say we're not alone.
Still some just wait the telephone
to ring and hear a friendly voice:
"It's Christmas time, time to rejoice."

Contrasts of Have and Have-Nots

26. The Gift That I Want Most

An orphan child, a refugee,
no home, also no family.
No family's gathered 'round a tree
that's filled with gifts for all to see.

But gifts are not what I desire,
for Christmas does not mean "acquire."
Maybe a toy's a lovely thought,
but what I want cannot be bought.

I'd like to be in a clean place
where I would see a friendly face.
On Christmas morning that would be
the gift that I'd most want for me.

Contrasts of Wanting, Needing, Waiting

27. To Want, Need, Wait

Wanting, needing, waiting—
    three agonizing words
can be quite frustrating
    or misery in thirds.

Who wants, needs, waits this year,
    this year at Christmas time—
rich with or without cheer
    and those without a dime?

Those who have—want, need, wait
    expensive gifts to find.
The "have-nots" need and wait;
    they have no gift in mind.

That is, no gift to buy,
    for food, water will do.
The wealthy wonder why
    the poor folks seem so blue.

Contrasts of Family

28. Our Family

Our family gathers year by year
    when Christmas time comes 'round.
If weather's fair or it turns drear,
    together they'll be found.

With grandpa, grandma this began
    with seven girls and boys,
and I, a grandson, was a fan
    of all the Christmas joys.

We gathered just for family,
    and O, what fun we had.
We grandchildren quite happily
    ate fruitcake, were we glad!

Our grand-folks' children (uncles, aunts)
    were quite a fun-filled crew;
they made sure we all had a chance
    to sing songs that we knew.

Though most of them were Christmas songs,
    that is without a doubt;
we knew where every beat belongs,
    in "You'd better watch out."

Our uncles sometimes sang quartets;
    our aunts would also sing.
The pianist no one forgets,
    my mom played everything.

We ate, we sang, an uncle prayed
    with thanks for us and food.
We cousins ate, sang, and then played;
    the sweets we ate—so good!

I'm thankful for a family
    that each year takes the time
to gather, I say gratefully,
    "Our family is sublime!"

I'm thankful for a family
    that gathers every year
to them I say most gratefully,
    "Next year I'll see you here."

Contrasts of Tradition(s)

29. Tradition(s)

In a few weeks Christmas is here
when bright lights, colors will appear.
With ornaments we'll deck our tree,
a time for joy, don't you agree?
Mom's Christmas cookies, what delight!
I'll savor each one, every bite.
There's Grandma's star of Bethlehem,
she purchased in Jerusalem.

The crèche also that Grandpa made,
which Mary, Joseph, Christ portrayed,
we've kept until the present day.
It seems he carved it yesterday.
Do we still have that string of lights
with those round bulbs in reds and whites?
We'll need some swags of holly, pine;
how nicely both of these combine.

Our family's changed across the years,
but each tradition always cheers.
The mem'ries of our family's past
each generation should hold fast.
An ornament ninety years old
was made by great grandpa, I'm told.
It's just a cow carved for the scene
of Jesus' birth each year we've seen.

Not special? Oh yes, special still.
He shaped it with his hands and will,
shaped by someone I never knew.
But this year I will keep in view
his little cow upon our tree
and think, "Great grandpa, you will see
I hope to learn to carve on wood
the way that my great grandpa could."

Contrasts of Christmas Memories

30. Christmas Memory

The smells, the sights of Christmas time,
the lighted trees and bells that chime,
the sweets my mother always baked,
the fun the morning I awaked,
the Christmas morn's the one I mean,
when tinsel, lights, and gifts were seen;
that's when I saw around the tree
the gift that someone left for me.
This memory gives me great joy;
a memory I still enjoy!

Contrasts of Children's Desires

31. Remembering Christmas

I sit alone at Christmas time
   remembering the past,
when living in a colder clime
   the cold days long would last.

The snow might fall to the delight
   of our four growing boys.
One year a foot of snowy white
   filled them with endless joys.

So they then built a large igloo
   with doors for in and out,
a rooftop with a chimney flue,
   an int'resting layout.

How wondrous Christmas memories:
   each child, each carol, tree,
especially grandpa's hand-carved star,
   a gift when I was three.

Contrasts of Christmas Kitchens

32. Mother's Fruitcakes

The fruitcakes that my mother made
    for Christmas time each year,
whose sweet aromas would not fade,
    would last till the New Year.

She made each one with loving care,
    ingredients cherry, green;
the batter, O its taste was rare,
    the best that's ever been.

The batter bowl, now there's a treat;
    I'd run my fingers round
and try to catch a lot to eat
    without making a sound.

I'd rather have a fruitcake slice
    from mother's Christmas cakes,
than pay a bakery's highest price
    for one the baker bakes.

Contrasts of Christmas Wishes

33. The Best Christmas Gift

At Christmas children wish for toys,
    perhaps new games to play.
Yet many children have few joys,
    no gifts on Christmas day.
The point is not to exclude toys
    from Yule celebrations.
It's rather to bring hopes and joys
    to each child, all nations.

In camps now filled with refugees
    and children who are poor,
who suffer hunger and disease,
    whose lives are most unsure,
what if we'd give them goodwill, peace,
    provide food, shelter, care?
What if we local wars could cease,
    a gift beyond compare?

Contrasts of Christmas Gifts

34. My Best Gift

A holiday, a holy day,
    a marriage day, and a birthday,
are times we sing, are times we pray,
    and yet our lifetimes slip away.

Our holidays go by so fast
    that first new doll, that first new train,
And quickly fifty years have passed
    and here my birthday comes again.

The holy days are special too,
    the calendar each year's so full,
so many, I can't keep in view,
    but each one has its special pull.

We like to say, "Treasure each day,"
    but that is sadly so cliché.
To friends and family we should say:
    "You are my best gift every day!"

Contrasts of a Child's Christmas

35. A Child's Christmas

In a few days Christmas is here,
when lights with colors will appear.
With ornaments we'll deck our tree,
each member of our family.

Mom's Christmas cookies, what delight!
I'll savor each one, every bite.
We'll hang a wreath on our front door,
the house we'll deck with Yule décor.

When grandma comes, she'll bring a cake,
that means momma won't have to bake.
My grandpa made a brand new sled
and hung it last week in our shed.

The forecast says, "Snow Christmas Day."
I'll test the sled without delay.
I've heard white Christmases are fun;
I'll give the sled its first test run.

Contrasts of Anticipation and Disappointment

36. The Christmas Card

A Christmas card I found this year
    was postmarked eighty years ago;
the postmark was not very clear;
    I think the town was Buffalo.

It fell behind my grandma's desk,
    and was not found for eighty years.
perhaps it seems a bit grotesque
    but its sad loss brings me to tears.

I opened it, saw grandpa's script,
    and wondered if he'd once been there,
until I saw inside he'd clipped
    his train receipt from where to where.

From Birmingham to Buffalo,
    my grandpa traveled there by train.
But there was no way he could know
    some plans of his would be in vain.

"Hi, Merry Christmas," said the card,
    "I have some news, very sad news,
and writing this is very hard;
    It turns my Christmas cheer to blues.

"The teachers' conference closed today
    and snow in sheets fell everywhere.
It is so cold, snow's here to stay.
    The drifts are high, beyond compare.

"I'm sad that I'll miss Christmas Day;
    for three more days the trains won't run.
A hotel room is where I'll stay,
    and here I'll miss the festive fun.

"But I'll phone you on Christmas Day.
    to wish you all much Christmas cheer,
Virginia, Jane, Mark, Fred, and May.
    I love you more with each New Year."

This card addressed to Grandma May,
    she never saw before she died,
But Grandpa's card shows me a way
    to share one's love; how Grandpa tried!

Contrasts of Christmas Music

37. Overwhelming Joy

The Christmas carols, rhythms, rhymes
on Christmas Eve join church bell chimes
to celebrate the Christ Child's birth
in many lands across the earth.

Some dance and sing in bright array,
while others simply sing and pray.
The languages are quite diverse.
It matters not from verse to verse.

The rhythms, melodies reveal
how Christmas in our hearts we feel.
They're jubilant, quite buoyant, still
and every year my heart they fill.

They fill with overwhelming joy
the hearts of every girl and boy,
who sing the story of the birth
of Christ who spreads love o'er the earth.

Contrasts of Christmas Eve

38. An Alpine Christmas Eve

A chapel on an alpine hill
    on Christmas Eve was dressed in snow.
The pastor wondered—Will it fill
    by midnight, candles all aglow?

Will snow-storm winds hold back the crowd
    of worshipers on Christmas Eve?
The pastor pondered with head bowed
    and dared not then the chapel leave.

Before the coming midnight hour,
    he thought he heard a Christmas hymn
waft faintly through the strong snow show'r
    to praise the Child of Bethlehem.

At midnight hour the chapel filled
    with carolers, fam'lies, and friends,
and sounds of Christmas Eve all thrilled.
    The joys of Christmas knew no ends.

Contrasts of Neighborhoods

39. Christmas Light(s)

The Christmas lights at city park
    shed light upon a nearby street,
where poverty has left its mark,
    and run-down homes are never neat.

The sidewalks are in ill repair,
    the street itself has ugly holes.
It seems the city does not care.
    Are neighbors seen to be lost souls?

Will Christmas lights shed the most light
    that this street will have all the year?
Will they expose a ghetto blight,
    the reasons children there have fear?

In other places, Christmas light
    will show to all love and goodwill,
but in this neighborhood at night
    compassion fails and all is ill.

Contrasts of Gain and Loss at Christmas

40. Christmas Gain and Loss

The bells, the lights, and carol sings,
which every Christmas season brings,
the holly, ivy, Christmas trees,
the cookies, cakes that always please,
are but a sign that we need cheer,
or they're just motions year on year.

But even routine cheer's not bad,
for few folks know the year you've had.
Still, Christmas never is routine;
each year there is a different scene:
Another child, grandchild is born,
another loved one that we mourn.

No Christmas story is the same,
and yet the Christ Child that we name
remains the same from year to year
The story of his birth we hear,
and though to some it may seem strange,
it has a power the world to change.

Epilogue

41. Contrasts of Christmas

Brightly decorated homes,
bleak dwellings of the poor.
Well-dressed holiday shoppers,
street children dressed in rags.
Bright tree lights and baubles,
Ukrainian homes without power.
Joyful, well-fed carolers,
hungry, crying children.
The Christ Child born in a stall,
poinsettia-graced churches.
Shepherds from the fields,
Wise Men from the East.
Wealth of Christmas industry,
poverty of the Christ-Child.
Gift-laden Christmas trees,
homeless children with nothing.
Purchase of Christmas gifts,
God's gift of the Christ-Child.
Economic success of Christmas sales,
God's concern for the well-being of all.

Name and Subject Index